MAKING MONEY ONLINE: BOOK 2

BY MICHAEL CALLUM MAYAKA

Brought to you by MCM Publications
(books.michaelmayaka.co.uk)

E-COMMERCE AND ONLINE RETAIL

FOREWORD:

In today's digital age, making money online has become a viable and accessible option for individuals seeking financial independence or additional income streams. The internet offers a plethora of opportunities that allow you to leverage your skills, creativity, and resources to generate revenue. This guide aims to provide you with valuable insights, strategies, and practical tips on how to make money online effectively.

This book is part of a series for more information see Further reading at the end of this book.

Table of Contents

Foreword: 4

2. E-commerce and Online Retail 7

    2.1 Setting up an Online Store: A Guide to E-commerce Success . 8

        1. Choose the Right E-commerce Platform: 9

        2. Define Your Products and Target Audience: 9

        3. Create an Engaging Website: 10

        4. Implement Secure Payment Options: 11

        5. Develop a Marketing Strategy: 11

        6. Optimize for Search Engines: 12

        7. Provide Excellent Customer Service: 13

        8. Monitor and Analyze Performance: 13

        9. Continuously Adapt and Improve: 14

        Conclusion: 14

    2.2 Dropshipping and Fulfillment by Amazon (FBA): Streamlining E-commerce Success 16

        Dropshipping: 17

        Benefits of Dropshipping: 17

        Fulfillment by Amazon (FBA): 19

        Benefits of FBA: 20

        Combining Dropshipping and FBA: 22

        Conclusion: 22

    2.3 Creating and Selling Digital Products 24

    2.4 Affiliate Marketing and Influencer Partnerships: Harnessing the Power of Online Influence 31

        Affiliate Marketing: 32

        Influencer Partnerships: 34

        Conclusion: 37

Further reading: 39

2. E-COMMERCE AND ONLINE RETAIL

2.1 SETTING UP AN ONLINE STORE: A GUIDE TO E-COMMERCE SUCCESS

In today's digital age, setting up an online store has become an increasingly popular way to start a business and reach a global customer base. The internet provides entrepreneurs with endless opportunities to showcase and sell their products or services. This section will guide you through the fundamental steps involved in setting up an online store.

1. CHOOSE THE RIGHT E-COMMERCE PLATFORM:

Selecting the right e-commerce platform is crucial for the success of your online store. Consider factors such as ease of use, customization options, scalability, payment gateways, and customer support. Popular platforms like Shopify, WooCommerce, and BigCommerce offer user-friendly interfaces, extensive features, and robust support, making them ideal choices for beginners.

2. DEFINE YOUR PRODUCTS AND TARGET AUDIENCE:

Before launching your online store, clearly define the products or services you will offer. Conduct market research to identify your target audience, their preferences, and buying behaviours. This will help you tailor your offerings and marketing strategies to attract and engage the right customers.

3. CREATE AN ENGAGING WEBSITE:

Design a visually appealing and user-friendly website that reflects your brand identity. Choose an appropriate colour scheme, high-quality product images, and clear product descriptions. Optimize your website for mobile devices, as an increasing number of users shop through smartphones and tablets.

4. IMPLEMENT SECURE PAYMENT OPTIONS:

Integrate secure and reliable payment gateways to provide customers with a seamless and trustworthy checkout experience. Popular options include PayPal, Stripe, and Square. Ensure that your website has an SSL certificate to encrypt customer data and protect sensitive information.

5. DEVELOP A MARKETING STRATEGY:

A well-executed marketing strategy is essential for driving traffic and generating sales. Leverage various digital marketing channels, such as search engine optimization (SEO), social media marketing, email marketing, and paid advertising. Create compelling content, engage with your audience, and leverage influencers to boost brand awareness and conversions.

6. OPTIMIZE FOR SEARCH ENGINES:

Implement SEO techniques to improve your online store's visibility in search engine results. Conduct keyword research and optimize your product pages, meta tags, and URLs. Generate high-quality backlinks to increase your website's authority and credibility.

7. PROVIDE EXCELLENT CUSTOMER SERVICE:

Deliver exceptional customer service to build trust and foster long-term relationships. Offer multiple channels for customer support, including email, live chat, and phone. Respond promptly to inquiries, address concerns, and resolve issues promptly and efficiently.

8. MONITOR AND ANALYZE PERFORMANCE:

Regularly monitor and analyze your online store's performance using analytics tools. Track metrics such as website traffic, conversion rates, and customer behaviour. Use this data to make informed decisions, optimize your marketing efforts, and improve your overall store performance.

9. CONTINUOUSLY ADAPT AND IMPROVE:

The online marketplace is constantly evolving, so it's crucial to stay updated and adapt to changing trends and customer preferences. Keep an eye on industry developments, embrace new technologies, and regularly update your product offerings and website to provide the best possible user experience.

CONCLUSION:

Setting up an online store requires careful planning, attention to detail, and continuous effort. By choosing the right e-commerce platform, defining your target audience, creating an engaging website, implementing secure payment options, and developing a robust marketing strategy, you can establish a successful online store. Remember to provide exceptional customer service, monitor performance metrics, and continuously adapt to meet the evolving needs of your customers. With dedication and perseverance, your online store can become a profitable venture in the vast realm of e-commerce.

2.2 DROPSHIPPING AND FULFILLMENT BY AMAZON (FBA): STREAMLINING E-COMMERCE SUCCESS

Dropshipping and Fulfillment by Amazon (FBA) are two popular models within the e-commerce industry that have revolutionized the way people do business online. These methods offer entrepreneurs and aspiring online retailers the opportunity to start their own businesses without the need for extensive inventory or warehousing capabilities. In this section, we will explore the key concepts and benefits of dropshipping and FBA.

DROPSHIPPING:

Dropshipping is a business model where the retailer does not keep products in stock. Instead, when a customer places an order, the retailer purchases the product from a third-party supplier who then directly ships it to the customer. The retailer acts as a middleman, facilitating the transaction and earning a profit on the price difference between the wholesale and retail price.

BENEFITS OF DROPSHIPPING:

1. Low startup costs: Dropshipping eliminates the need for significant upfront investments in inventory, storage, or fulfilment infrastructure, making it an

attractive option for entrepreneurs on a limited budget.

2. Wide product selection: With dropshipping, you have access to an extensive range of products from various suppliers. This allows you to offer a diverse catalogue without the hassle of managing inventory.

3. Location independence: As a dropshipper, you can run your business from anywhere with an internet connection. There are no limitations imposed by physical store locations or warehousing requirements.

4. Flexibility and scalability: Dropshipping allows you to test new products and markets easily. You can quickly add or remove

products from your store based on demand, enabling you to scale your business efficiently.

FULFILLMENT BY AMAZON (FBA):

Fulfillment by Amazon (FBA) is a program offered by Amazon that simplifies the order fulfilment process for e-commerce sellers. Under the FBA model, sellers send their products to Amazon's fulfilment centres, and Amazon takes care of storage, packing, shipping, and customer service. When a customer places an order, Amazon handles the entire logistics process.

BENEFITS OF FBA:

1. Prime eligibility: Products fulfilled by Amazon are eligible for Prime two-day shipping, which can significantly increase your product's visibility and chances of conversion.

2. Trusted customer service: Amazon's customer service team handles inquiries, returns, and refunds, providing excellent support to your customers.

3. Efficient logistics: With FBA, you leverage Amazon's robust logistics infrastructure, allowing you to focus on other aspects of your business, such as marketing and product sourcing.

4. Multi-channel fulfilment: FBA extends beyond Amazon's platform. You can use

the FBA program to fulfil orders from other e-commerce platforms, further expanding your customer reach.

COMBINING DROPSHIPPING AND FBA:

Some entrepreneurs choose to combine dropshipping and FBA to create a hybrid business model. In this approach, they utilize dropshipping for products not available through FBA or for testing new products. For high-demand or profitable products, they leverage FBA to benefit from Amazon's logistics network and Prime eligibility.

CONCLUSION:

Dropshipping and Fulfillment by Amazon (FBA) are powerful e-commerce models that have empowered countless entrepreneurs to start their own businesses with minimal upfront investment. Dropshipping provides flexibility and a wide product selection, while FBA offers streamlined logistics and the advantages of selling on the Amazon platform. By understanding and implementing these models effectively, you can tap into the immense potential of e-commerce and build a successful online business.

2.3 CREATING AND SELLING DIGITAL PRODUCTS

In the digital age, the demand for digital products has soared, presenting a lucrative opportunity for individuals to create and sell their own digital offerings. Digital products are intangible goods that can be downloaded, accessed, or consumed online, ranging from e-books and online courses to software, graphics, and music. This section will explore the process of creating and selling digital products, highlighting key steps and considerations for success.

1. Idea Generation: The first step in creating a digital product is to generate a compelling and marketable idea. Consider your

expertise, passion, and the needs of your target audience. Research popular trends, identify gaps in the market, and brainstorm ideas that align with your skills and interests.

2. Planning and Research: Once you have an idea, conduct thorough research to validate its viability and potential profitability. Analyze your target market, competition, and pricing strategies. Identify the unique selling points of your digital product and determine how it will provide value to customers.

3. Content Creation: With a solid plan in place, it's time to create your digital product. Depending on the type of product, this

could involve writing an e-book, recording video tutorials for an online course, designing graphics, or developing software. Focus on delivering high-quality content that is informative, engaging, and visually appealing.

4. Packaging and Presentation: How you package and present your digital product plays a crucial role in attracting customers. Create professional-looking covers, thumbnails, or product images that accurately represent your offering. Pay attention to branding and ensure consistency across all elements.

5. Platform Selection: Choosing the right platform to sell your digital product is vital. Several options are available, including self-hosted platforms, online marketplaces, and digital product marketplaces. Consider factors such as ease of use, payment processing, security, and audience reach when selecting a platform.

6. Sales and Marketing: Developing an effective marketing strategy is essential to drive sales and generate awareness for your digital product. Leverage various marketing channels, such as social media, email marketing, content marketing, and paid advertising, to promote your product. Engage with your target audience, provide

valuable insights, and build a community around your brand.

7. Pricing and Monetization: Set a competitive and profitable price for your digital product. Consider factors such as production costs, perceived value, market demand, and customer preferences. Experiment with different pricing models, such as one-time payments, subscriptions, or tiered pricing structures, to find the best fit for your product and target audience.

8. Delivery and Customer Support: Ensure a smooth and seamless delivery process for your digital product. Set up automated systems to handle payments, downloads,

and access to online courses or software. Provide clear instructions and support to customers, addressing any queries or technical issues promptly.

9. Continuous Improvement: To stay competitive, continually improve and update your digital product based on customer feedback and evolving market trends. Seek customer reviews and testimonials to build trust and credibility. Consider launching new versions or complementary products to expand your offering.

10. Intellectual Property Protection: Safeguard your digital product by

implementing copyright protection, watermarking, or licensing agreements. Research legal requirements and consult professionals to ensure compliance with intellectual property laws.

Creating and selling digital products can be a highly profitable venture, offering flexibility and scalability. With careful planning, quality content, effective marketing, and attentive customer support, you can establish a successful online business and generate sustainable income from your digital creations. Embrace your creativity, tap into market demands, and seize the opportunities presented by the digital world.

2.4 AFFILIATE MARKETING AND INFLUENCER PARTNERSHIPS: HARNESSING THE POWER OF ONLINE INFLUENCE

Affiliate marketing and influencer partnerships have emerged as highly effective strategies for monetizing online platforms and harnessing the power of online influence. These methods allow individuals and businesses to leverage the reach and credibility of influencers to promote products or services and earn commissions for successful referrals. In this section, we will delve into the world of affiliate marketing and influencer partnerships, exploring their benefits, best practices, and how to get started.

AFFILIATE Marketing:

Affiliate marketing is a performance-based marketing model where affiliates earn a commission for driving traffic or sales to a merchant's website through their unique referral links. The affiliate acts as a middleman, connecting the target audience with products or services that align with their interests or needs. Here are some key aspects of affiliate marketing:

1. Affiliate Networks: Joining an affiliate network, such as Amazon Associates,

ClickBank, or ShareASale, provides access to a wide range of products and affiliate programs. These networks facilitate the tracking of referrals, commission payouts, and provide marketing materials.

2. Niche Selection: To maximize success, it's crucial to choose a niche that aligns with your expertise and audience's interests. Focusing on a specific niche allows you to establish authority and credibility, increasing the likelihood of conversions.

3. Content Creation: Creating valuable and engaging content, such as product reviews, tutorials, or comparison articles, helps build trust with your audience. Incorporate your

affiliate links naturally within the content to encourage clicks and conversions.

4. Promotional Channels: Promote your affiliate links through various channels, such as your blog, social media profiles, email newsletters, or YouTube videos. Tailor your promotional efforts to each platform's audience and utilize effective marketing techniques.

INFLUENCER PARTNERSHIPS:

Influencer partnerships involve collaborating with individuals who have a significant online following and influence over their audience. These influencers can range from social media personalities to bloggers, vloggers, or industry experts. Here's how to make the most of influencer partnerships:

1. Finding the Right Influencers: Research and identify influencers whose audience aligns with your target market. Look for individuals with high engagement rates, a genuine connection with their audience, and content that resonates with your brand.

2. Establishing Relationships: Approach influencers with a personalized pitch, highlighting the mutual benefits of collaborating. Building a genuine relationship based on trust and mutual

respect lays the foundation for a successful partnership.

3. Clear Expectations: Clearly define the terms of the partnership, including deliverables, compensation, and disclosure requirements. Establishing expectations upfront helps ensure a smooth collaboration and avoids any misunderstandings.

4. Creative Campaigns: Work together with influencers to develop creative and engaging campaigns that promote your products or services. Give influencers creative freedom while aligning the campaign with your brand values and goals.

5. Tracking and Analytics: Implement tracking tools to measure the success of the influencer campaign. Track key performance indicators such as reach, engagement, conversions, and ROI to assess the effectiveness of the partnership.

CONCLUSION:

Affiliate marketing and influencer partnerships offer powerful ways to leverage online influence and drive revenue. By tapping into the networks of influencers or becoming an affiliate marketer, individuals and businesses can expand their reach, increase brand awareness, and drive conversions. Remember, building strong relationships, creating valuable content, and choosing the right partners are key elements of successful affiliate marketing and influencer partnerships. With careful planning and strategic execution, these methods can become valuable revenue streams in your online money-making journey.

FURTHER READING:

If you enjoyed this book, please consider reading one of the other books in the series:

Making Money Online: Book 1 (Understanding the Online Landscape)

Making Money Online: Book 2 (E-commerce and Online Retail)

Making Money Online: Book 3 (Freelancing and Remote Work)

Making Money Online: Book 4 (Content Creation and Monetization)

Making Money Online: Book 5 (Online Tutoring and Education)

Making Money Online: Book 6 (Online Surveys, Microtasks, and Rewards)

Making Money Online: Book 7 (Online Investments and Trading)

Making Money Online: Book 8 (Creating and Selling Digital Assets)

Making Money Online: Book 9 (Online Consulting and Coaching)

Making Money Online: Book 10 (Maximizing Online Income Opportunities)

All the books can be found on Amazon as Kindle and Paperback, or you can buy the complete edition which contains the full series in one book. The complete edition is available as Kindle, Paperback and exclusively as Hardback. You can find all the links in my book site: books.michaelmayaka.co.uk.

www.ingramcontent.com/pod-product-compliance
Lightning Source LLC
Chambersburg PA
CBHW040254220526
45473CB00001B/476